Natural Disasters

VOLCANOES

JACQUELINE DINEEN

FRANKLIN WATTS
LONDON • SYDNEY

CONTENTS

ASKC

VOLCANOES

© Aladdin Books Ltd 2002

Designed and produced by
Aladdin Books Ltd
28 Percy Street
London W1T 2BZ

Revised and updated edition published in 2002
First published in Great Britain in 1991 by
Franklin Watts
96 Leonard Street
London EC2A 4XD

Design: David West
            Children's Book Design
Designer: Stephen Woosnam-Savage
Editors: Fiona Robertson
            Libby Volke
Illustrator: Aziz Khan
Picture Researchers: Emma Krikler
                            Brian Hunter Smart
Consultant: Martin Bramwell

ISBN 0 7496 4404 4 (hardcover)
ISBN 0 7496 4807 4 (paperback)
A CIP catalogue record for this book is available
from the British Library.

Printed in UAE

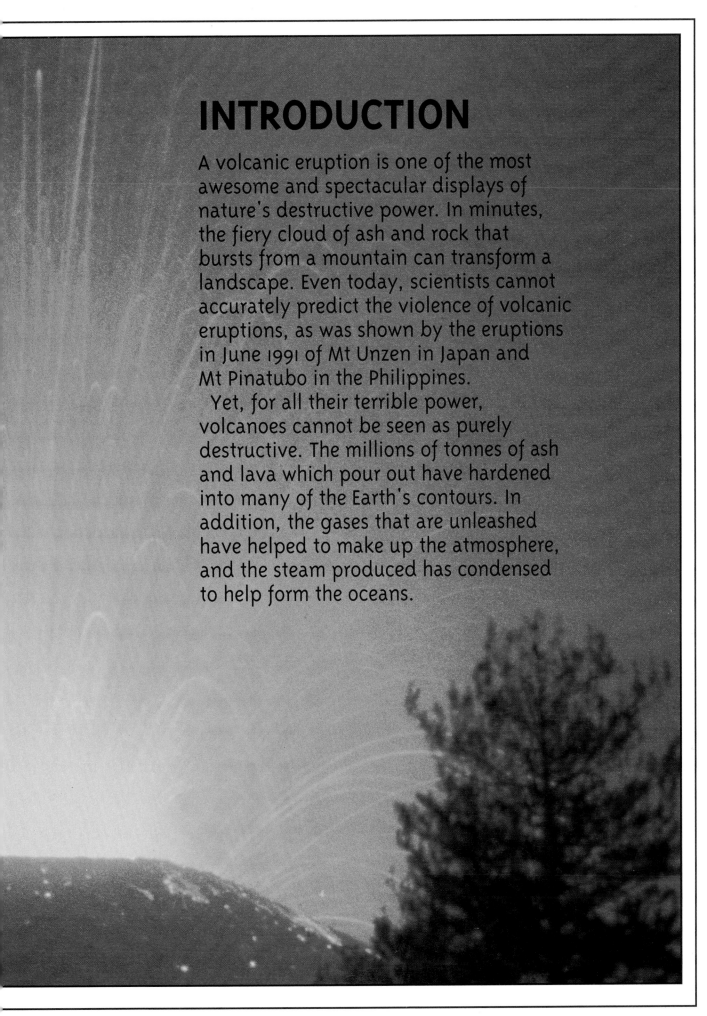

INTRODUCTION

A volcanic eruption is one of the most awesome and spectacular displays of nature's destructive power. In minutes, the fiery cloud of ash and rock that bursts from a mountain can transform a landscape. Even today, scientists cannot accurately predict the violence of volcanic eruptions, as was shown by the eruptions in June 1991 of Mt Unzen in Japan and Mt Pinatubo in the Philippines.

Yet, for all their terrible power, volcanoes cannot be seen as purely destructive. The millions of tonnes of ash and lava which pour out have hardened into many of the Earth's contours. In addition, the gases that are unleashed have helped to make up the atmosphere, and the steam produced has condensed to help form the oceans.

WHAT IS A VOLCANO?

Volcanoes are openings in the surface of the Earth, from which molten rock, called magma, and gases can escape.

The Earth is made up of three layers — the crust, the mantle and the core. The crust is the outermost layer of rock and can be quite thin. The continental crust is between 30 and 50 km thick, but the oceanic crust is only about 5 km thick.

The crust feels solid, but it consists of giant plates (see illustration, right) which float on the upper mantle. The upper mantle is made of hot, molten rock called magma, which is always moving. Pressure in the mantle forces magma to the surface.

Volcanic eruptions occur where the rising magma finds a way through a crack or weakness in the Earth's crust, usually at the edges of plates. These are called plate margins.

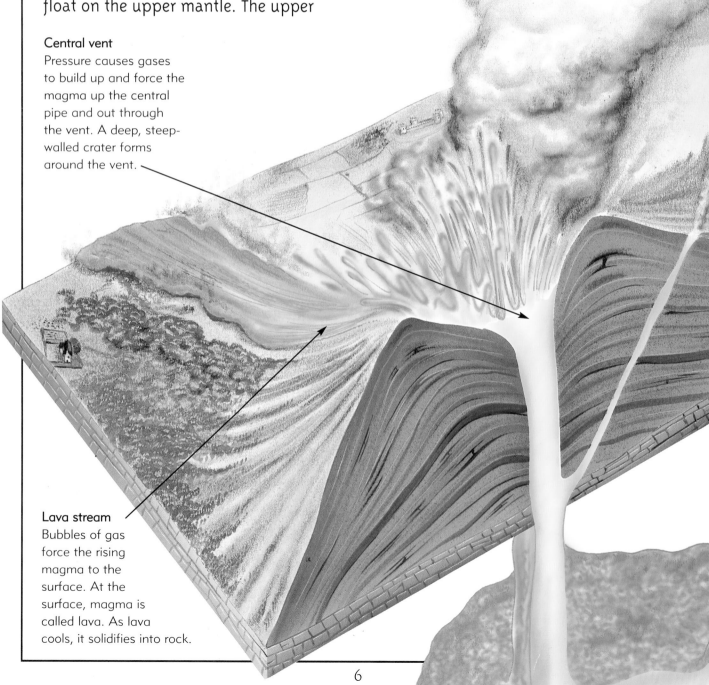

Central vent
Pressure causes gases to build up and force the magma up the central pipe and out through the vent. A deep, steep-walled crater forms around the vent.

Lava stream
Bubbles of gas force the rising magma to the surface. At the surface, magma is called lava. As lava cools, it solidifies into rock.

Layers

The steep slopes are built up of alternate layers of ash and hardened lava. Sometimes lava bursts through in other places and forms 'parasitic' cones on the sides of the main cone.

Ash

The clouds of ash and gas that pour from the volcano help to form the cone shape around its vent. The ash consists of tiny pieces of lava, which harden into rock called tuff.

Magma

Magma collects in a chamber in the upper mantle. It is formed when two plates collide. The edge of one plate is dragged down under the other and melts into magma.

Plate movements

200 million years ago, all the land was joined together in one big continent called Pangaea. Gradually, the pieces drifted apart and formed the seven continents we have today. Active volcanoes are usually found in definite zones, near plate margins. They are mostly caused by plate movement.

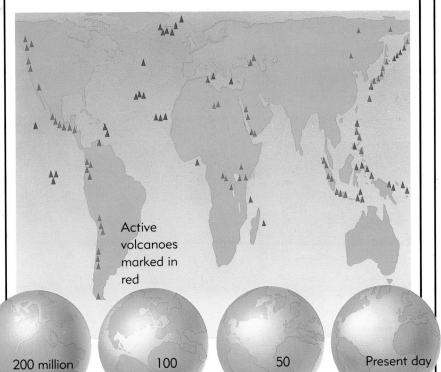

Active volcanoes marked in red

200 million years ago	100	50	Present day

Types of volcano

Thick, slow-moving andesite lava builds up high, cone-shaped volcanoes. Andesite volcanoes are very violent.

Shield volcanoes form when runny lava escapes through a fissure and flows a long way. The volcano has broad sloping sides like a shield.

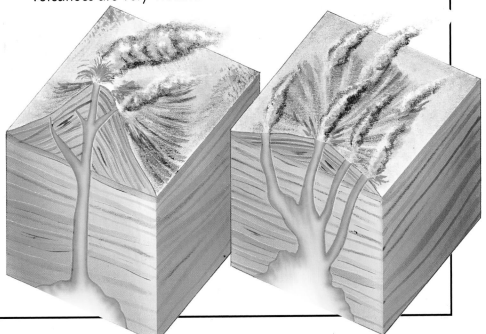

ACTIVE OR EXTINCT?

Active volcanoes are ones that still erupt. They occur mainly at the edges of the Earth's plates, where new crust is being formed, and old crust is destroyed. Of the 500 active volcanoes in the world, 20 to 30 erupt each year, such as Nevado del Ruiz in Colombia, South America.

Dormant, or 'sleeping', volcanoes are the ones that are quiet for a long time and then suddenly erupt again. Two examples are Mount Fujiyama in Japan, which last erupted in 1707, and Mount Rainier in the United States, which has not erupted for over 100 years. Both these volcanoes still have lava bubbling in the crater and steam rising from them. No one knows when they may erupt again.

An extinct volcano is one that has not erupted for thousands of years. Mount Egmont in New Zealand and Mount Kilimanjaro in Tanzania, Africa, are extinct volcanoes. But even 'extinct' volcanoes can suddenly erupt, as Tristan da Cunha and Helgafell in Iceland showed!

↑ Mount Fujiyama in Hondo, Japan, has been dormant since 1707.

➝ Edinburgh Castle is built on the remains of a volcano which has been extinct for 325 million years.

➝ (Main picture) The eruption of Mauna Loa, on Hawaii. At 4,171 m high, it is the world's largest active volcano. Hawaii is the only island in the chain of Hawaiian Islands which still has active volcanoes.

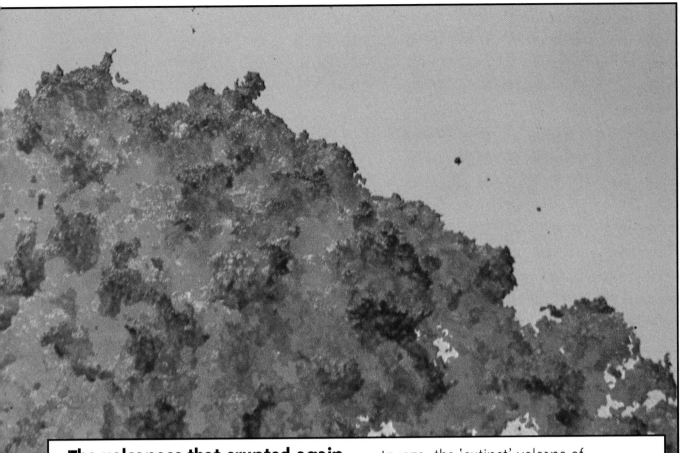

The volcanoes that erupted again

Tristan da Cunha (below) is a volcanic island in the South Atlantic Ocean which was believed to be extinct. In 1961, it suddenly erupted again. The 270 islanders escaped in boats.

In 1973, the 'extinct' volcano of Helgafell erupted on the Icelandic island of Heimaey. The people escaped, but many houses were buried or burnt by the red-hot lava flows that flowed towards the island's fishing port.

WHEN A VOLCANO ERUPTS

Volcanoes are, in a sense, the safety valves in the Earth's crust, releasing the build-up of pressure caused by gases beneath the Earth's surface.

The strength of a volcanic eruption depends on the type of magma and the amount of gases trapped in it. The magma formed when plates pull apart is very fluid. The gases in it have time to escape and there is no volcanic eruption. When plates collide, however, the magma formed is much thicker and stickier. Gases become trapped in it and escape explosively in a huge cloud of steam and dust thousands of metres high.

A volcano may be quiet for many years before it erupts again. Often its slopes are covered with grass and trees, like an ordinary mountain. A thin wisp of vapour rising from the crater may be the only sign that it is a still-active volcano.

Surges of red-hot lava flood out of the volcano's crater at speeds of up to 180 meters per second. Lava will flow from the volcano as long as there is enough pressure to force it to the surface. After such violent eruptions, the entire volcano often collapses into its empty magma chamber, forming a steep-sided depression called a caldera.

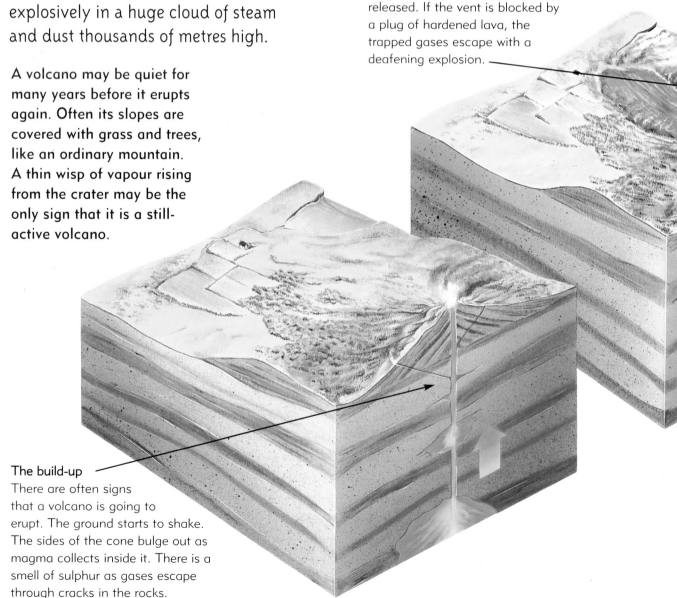

The explosion
When a volcano erupts, the gases dissolved in the magma are released. If the vent is blocked by a plug of hardened lava, the trapped gases escape with a deafening explosion.

The build-up
There are often signs that a volcano is going to erupt. The ground starts to shake. The sides of the cone bulge out as magma collects inside it. There is a smell of sulphur as gases escape through cracks in the rocks.

Afterwards

As well as lava and ash, the volcano belches out clouds of steam which condense into water. If there is a lot of steam, it falls as rain and mixes with the ash to form a thick mud. This may pour downhill, burying towns and villages.

↑ A fountain of molten lava erupts from a fissure in Hawaii's Kilauea volcano in 1983. Molten lava can reach temperatures of over 1,000 degrees centigrade. Mount Etna in Italy erupted throughout July and August 2001. Lava flows from a vent 2,100 m up the mountain partially destroyed a cable car station and a main road. Mount Mayon in the Philippines also erupted in July 2001, spewing lava 60 m into the air, and belching massive ash clouds.

→ A 'plastic' skin often forms over fast-flowing, runny lava. The skin is dragged into picturesque folds by the still-liquid lava running beneath it.

VOLCANOES UNDER THE SEA

The largest number of volcanoes is found under the sea floor. The ocean floor is very thin and can be easily pierced by the magma which lies underneath, especially along the lines of weakness at plate margins. One such plate margin runs down the Atlantic Ocean. When the plates move apart, rising magma seeps up into the gap and hardens into a new strip of crust. This makes the Atlantic wider, and therefore forces Europe and North America further apart.

The Earth is not getting bigger so, if new crust forms in one place, old crust must disappear in another.

More than half the world's volcanoes occur in a belt around the Pacific Ocean, known as the 'Ring of Fire'. They form when plate edges collide and old crust is dragged back into the mantle.

Sometimes volcanoes form when a crustal plate moves over a 'hotspot' in the Earth's mantle. Molten magma bores upwards from a fixed position deep below the ocean floor and breaks through the drifting plates to form shield volcanoes, like the Hawaiian Islands.

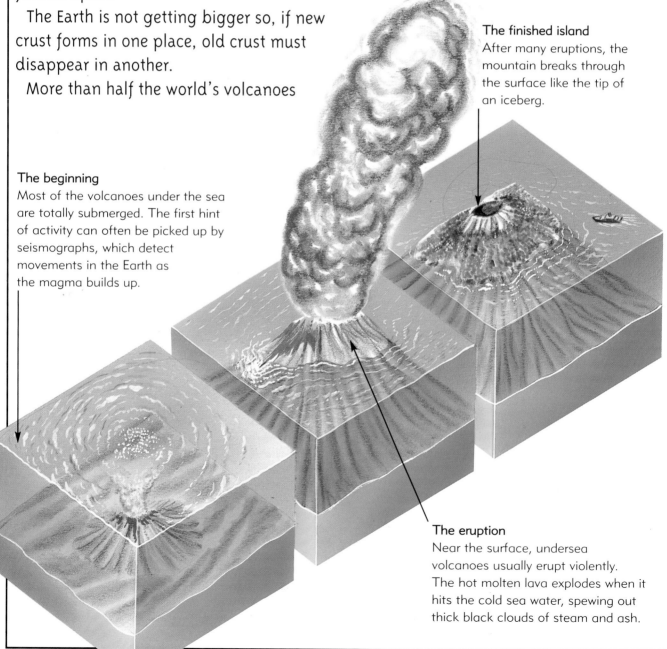

The finished island
After many eruptions, the mountain breaks through the surface like the tip of an iceberg.

The beginning
Most of the volcanoes under the sea are totally submerged. The first hint of activity can often be picked up by seismographs, which detect movements in the Earth as the magma builds up.

The eruption
Near the surface, undersea volcanoes usually erupt violently. The hot molten lava explodes when it hits the cold sea water, spewing out thick black clouds of steam and ash.

↓ Birds also help to carry seed to the new island.

↓ This picture shows recent lava formations around the crest of the East Pacific rise.

New life

At first the newly-created island is bare rock. Soil is formed from tiny bits of volcanic rock worn away by the wind and water. Seeds are carried there by the wind, and take root. Soon plants, like the cacti below, and insects flourish there.

VOLCANOES IN HISTORY

Today, the spectacular displays of energy produced by volcanoes provide clues to the Earth's evolution and the nature of its interior. But for thousands of years, people did not understand why a mountain suddenly burst apart and fiery liquid poured out. The effects of volcanoes were even more devastating than they are today, because people could not recognise the warning signs.

One of the most famous volcanic disasters was in AD 79, when Mount Vesuvius in southern Italy erupted. The volcano had been quiet for centuries. People farmed the land on the cone, and two important towns, Pompeii and Herculaneum, had grown up near its foot.

There had been earthquakes, but they were not seen as a sign that the volcano might erupt. One day, seemingly without warning, a massive explosion blew off the top of Vesuvius. The towns were buried in ash and more than 20,000 inhabitants were killed.

Pompeii
The thunderous eruption of Vesuvius left the surrounding countryside unrecognisable. Pompeii was buried under 6 m of ash, and steam and mud combined to form the torrent that engulfed Herculaneum in 16 m of volcanic mud.

↑↓ When archaeologists uncovered Pompeii, they found shapes of bodies preserved in hardened ash. Many of the victims had been choked by dust and gas.

Volcanoes in legend

The legend of Atlantis tells of a mighty island empire, described by the Greek philosopher Plato in 360 BC, which mysteriously disappeared into the sea.

Recent evidence suggests that Atlantis was on the Greek island of Thera, now known as Santorini, and that it was devastated in 1470 BC by one of the most powerful volcanic eruptions ever recorded. There were no survivors. When the volcano stopped erupting, its empty shell collapsed into a 180-m-deep crater in the sea, causing a massive tidal wave which destroyed most of nearby Crete.

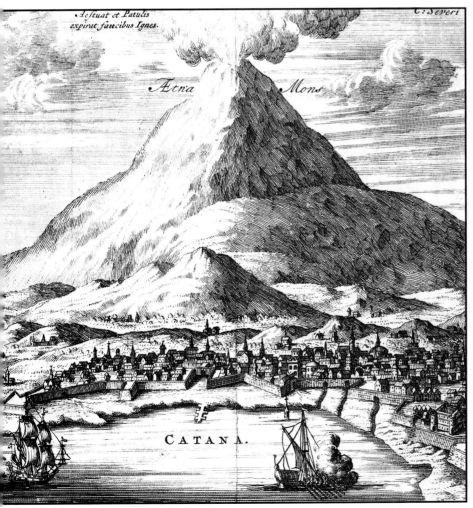

↑ Many volcanoes today are tourist attractions, such as the remains of Vesuvius (above).

← Mount Etna is situated on the island of Sicily. It is Europe's highest, most continuously active volcano. Etna has erupted at least 400 times in the last 2,500 years.

KRAKATAU ERUPTS

The loudest and most violent explosion in modern times was in 1883, when the uninhabited Indonesian island of Krakatau erupted and was almost completely destroyed. Krakatau was the stump of an old volcano, but it had not erupted for 200 years, and the central vent was blocked by a plug of solid lava. However, pressure was building up under the plug. Krakatau was getting ready to blow its top!

At 10:02 am on 27 August, the whole mountain erupted, ripping the island apart. The explosion was so loud it was heard in Australia, nearly 5,000 km away.

Rocks were thrown more than 50 km into the air. A massive cloud of ash darkened the skies for almost 500 km around.

The eruption caused a 35-m-high tidal wave, or *tsunami*, which destroyed 163 villages on nearby islands. More than 36,000 people were drowned.

The first signs
A series of small explosions occurring as gases began to escape. The volcano's walls collapsed, and steam built up as sea water poured onto the hot magma below.

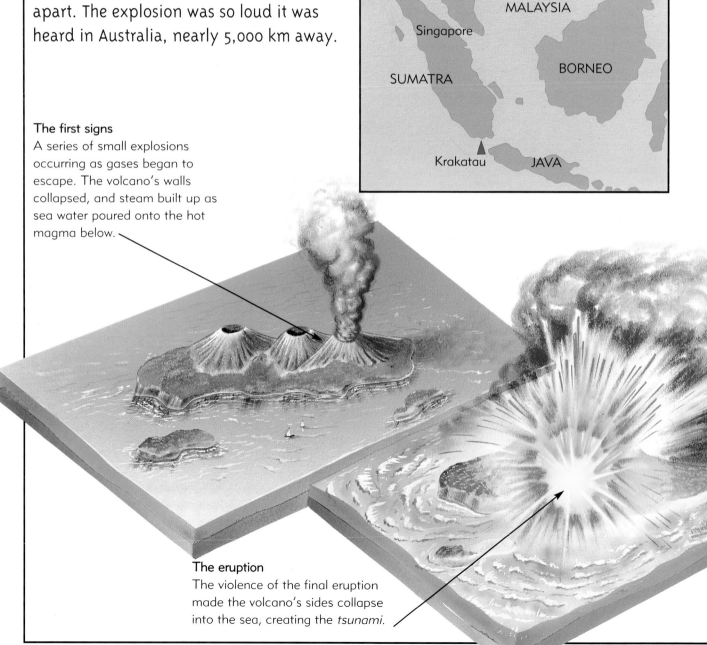

THE ERUPTION OF KRAKATAU

MALAYSIA

Singapore

SUMATRA

BORNEO

Krakatau   JAVA

The eruption
The violence of the final eruption made the volcano's sides collapse into the sea, creating the *tsunami*.

↑ An illustration of a steamer in Sumatra, beached by the tidal wave from the eruption of nearby Krakatau.

↓ Anak Krakatau. Evidence of recent lava flows can be seen here.

After the blast
The volcano was still active, and by 1927 a new island had been created called Anak Krakatau (Child of Krakatau).

MOUNT ST HELENS

Mount St Helens is a volcanic peak in the Cascade Mountains of Washington State, United States. On 18 May 1980, a huge explosion ripped the mountain apart, releasing clouds of ash and dust (below), which are still in the atmosphere.

Geologists knew that the volcano could erupt at any time. It had been dormant since 1857, but a series of small earthquakes during the 1970s suggested that magma was rising into the mountain. There were other warning signs too. The side of the mountain was bulging, and steam and gas were escaping.

At 8:32 am, an earthquake broke the bulging side loose, causing the worst landslide ever recorded. Rock and lava cascaded down the mountainside and clouds of hot gases and ash plunged the valley into darkness. The eruption killed 63 people, flattened forests and destroyed wildlife over 500 sq km.

The volcano continued to erupt violently for four days and there were smaller eruptions for several months.

Effect on the environment

After the eruption, the countryside around Mt St Helens resembled a desert of ash and charred remains (below). Five years later, however, wildlife could be found once again in the area. Other, more long-term effects have resulted from the 30 million tonnes of ash flung into the atmosphere (right) at the time of the explosion. The effect of the ash on the amount of sunlight reaching the ground may have caused changes in the weather worldwide.

NEW VOLCANOES

In 1943, a farmer from the village of Paricutín in Mexico noticed that a crack in his cornfield was getting longer. In February that year, the ground began to shake. Steam and gases poured out, and lava shot up into the air. By the end of the week, the cone was 150 metres high. In 1944, when the volcano was 500 m high, fiery lava flows destroyed a nearby town. The volcano continued to be active until 1952, by which time it was 2,770 m high.

Volcanic eruptions occur more frequently underwater than on land. In 1963, some fishermen saw clouds of smoke rising from the sea near Iceland. It was coming from a volcano on the sea bed. Soon steam and lava were being flung into the air. A day later, a small island had appeared above the surface. By the time the eruptions stopped, the highest point was over 170 metres above sea level. The new island was named Surtsey, after the Icelandic god of fire.

→↑ Surtsey erupted for several months. It gave scientists a rare chance to watch an island grow. When the eruptions stopped, the island covered 2.4 km.

→ Scientists could also study the development of life on the island. Plants began to grow only a few months after it had formed.

(Main picture) A cloud of steam and ash rises from the newborn island of Surtsey. For three years, Surtsey provided spectacular evidence of volcanic activity along the plate margins in the Atlantic Ocean.

CHANGING THE LANDSCAPE

One of the simplest ways volcanoes change the landscape is by forming new rock. Rock formed from hardened magma or lava is called igneous rock, from the Latin word *ignis*, meaning fire. The dark, runny lava which flows out of fissures hardens into an igneous rock called basalt. The lava from andesite volcanoes is lighter in colour because it contains large amounts of the mineral silica. If gas is trapped in the lava, it hardens into pumice, which is a very light rock filled with gas bubbles. Granite is a rough, grainy kind of igneous rock formed when magma cools in the crust.

↑ Layers of volcanic ash near Caldeira das Sete Cidades in the Azores.

↓← Pahoehoe, or ropy lava, has a smooth, twisted surface.

↓→ Crater Lake, USA. This water-filled caldera is now a national park.

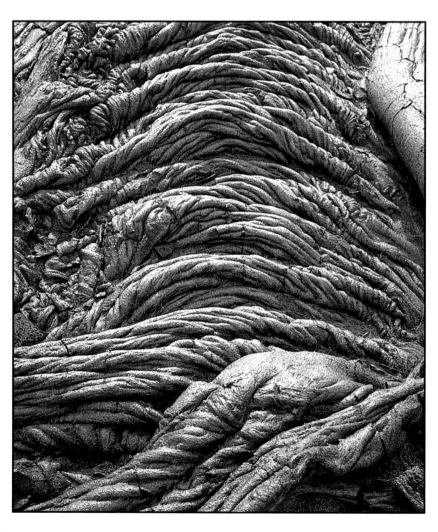

Mount Erebus

Mount Erebus is the only active volcano in Antarctica. It consists of three older craters, in addition to the current active one. The tip is covered with snow, but lava bubbles in the main crater. Steam which pours out from fumaroles, or openings in the ground, has frozen around the volcano's vent to form ice chimneys, which are over 20 metres in height.

Although there are no active volcanoes in Britain or France, ancient eruptions have left their mark on the landscape. Edinburgh Castle in Scotland and the chapel at Le Puy in France are both built on volcanic plugs of lava. The Giant's Causeway in Northern Ireland looks like huge stepping stones. The rocks are basalt formed from cooled lava of basalt.

Crater Lake sits on top of an extinct volcano in Oregon, USA. Despite its name, it is not a crater. When magma stops rising in a volcano, the top of the mountain may collapse into the empty magma chamber below, forming a deep, hollow caldera. Calderas are often filled by a lake. Crater Lake is 600 m deep and 9 km wide. The empty caldera of Ngorongoro Crater in Tanzania, Africa, is now a wildlife reserve.

DO VOLCANOES AFFECT US?

Many people near volcanoes live in fear of an eruption, which would force them to flee their homes. But can volcanoes affect us all?

When volcanoes erupt, they emit gases, including carbon dioxide and sulphur dioxide. Carbon dioxide is a greenhouse gas. This means that it helps to keep the Earth warm. In the past, the amount of carbon dioxide released by volcanoes helped to maintain the balance of gases in the atmosphere. However, this balance is now being upset. Burning fossil fuels and cutting down and burning trees both produce large amounts of carbon dioxide.

If too much carbon dioxide is trapped, temperatures around the world could go up.

The sulphur dioxide produced by volcanoes contributes to the problem of acid rain. When it mixes with water vapour in the air, it forms a very weak acid. This acid then falls to the ground in rain, snow or dust.

Industry
Factories and power stations burn coal, oil or gas and belch out smoke which contains carbon dioxide. Industry is a major cause of air pollution.

Homes and traffic
Home heating systems and motor vehicles burn fuels, producing carbon dioxide.

Destroying forests
Plants absorb carbon dioxide and release the oxygen we breathe. Huge areas of forest have been destroyed.

Transport
The nitrogen oxides in the exhaust fumes of aeroplanes add to pollution in the air.

Volcanoes

When volcanoes erupt, they emit gases which have been trapped underground. About one fifth of the sulphur dioxide in the air comes from volcanoes.

↑ Fine volcanic ash rising high into the atmosphere can produce beautiful sunsets. But large quantities of ash can also blot out sunlight.

Animal wastes

Cattle produce gases like methane during digestion. Methane is a greenhouse gas.

Acid rain

Acid rain is caused by sulphur dioxide and nitrogen oxides in the air.

The sulphur dioxide can kill trees, destroy buildings and poison life in ponds, rivers and lakes.

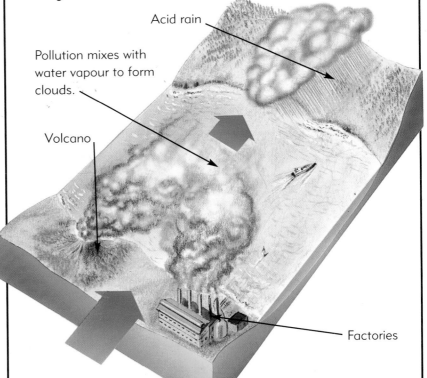

Acid rain

Pollution mixes with water vapour to form clouds.

Volcano

Factories

↑ This farm in Lanzarote is situated in the crater of an extinct volcano, where fertile soil provides ideal growing conditions.

← The heat from volcanoes makes metal in the crust melt and flow through cracks in the rocks, where they cool and solidify. Gold, shown left, is often mined from the remains of old volcanoes.

ARE VOLCANOES ALL BAD?

An active volcano may erupt at any time. Yet many farms and villages are built on slopes of volcanoes. So why do people take such risks?

One reason is that the soil is very fertile. In India, the ancient basalt lava flows from volcanic eruptions in the past have eroded into the rich black soil of the Deccan Plateau, where cotton is now grown. Farmers in Indonesia grow rice in volcanic soil, and there are vineyards and orange and lemon groves on the slopes of Mount Etna.

Geothermal energy, or energy from the Earth, is another vital resource of volcanic areas. It would take 20,000 times the world's coal supply to produce the heat that exists in the upper 11 km of the Earth's crust. Today, many geothermal power stations have been built in Iceland, New Zealand and Japan, where groundwater and magma provide hot water and steam. As supplies of fossil fuels run out, geothermal energy is a relatively clean and almost endless resource for the future.

Alternative energy

Water seeps through layers of porous rock, like limestone, until it meets a layer of impermeable rock, such as granite. The water collects in the tiny spaces between the grains of the rock, and is heated by the hot rocks of the volcano to produce steam. This steam is piped to power stations, where it is used to turn the turbines of an electricity generator. Geothermal energy can also provide heat for other sources, such as these greenhouses in Iceland, shown below.

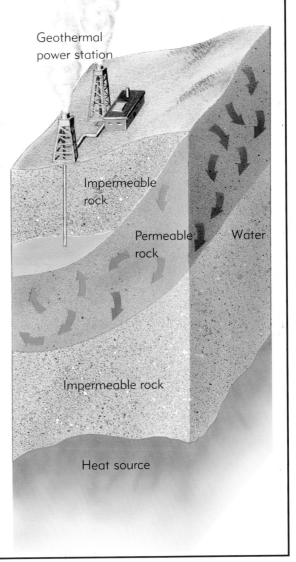

Geothermal power station

Impermeable rock

Permeable rock

Water

Impermeable rock

Heat source

WHAT CAN WE DO?

We cannot stop volcanoes erupting and we cannot prevent people from living near them and taking advantage of the fertile soil to grow their crops. So can we prevent future disasters where people are killed and towns destroyed?

Scientists try to give warnings about future eruptions so that people can be evacuated. They study movements in the rocks beneath the Earth's surface. Rising magma creates a series of tiny earthquakes which can be used as early warnings. The volcano's shape can also be monitored. As the magma chamber fills up, it begins to swell or bulge, which indicates that the volcano is on the verge of erupting.

However, to a large extent, volcanoes remain a mystery to science. Predicting eruptions is still an uncertain and dangerous business. In July 2000, two Indonesian volcanologists were killed, and several others were injured in an explosion at the summit crater of Semeru volcano in Java.

← Scientists use laser beams like these to help predict volcanic eruptions. A swelling on the volcano caused by the build-up of magma can be detected by a change in the length of the laser beam.

← ← Using a canvas glove to protect his hand from the heat, this volcanologist takes a sample of molten rock with a geological pick. By analysing samples, scientists can estimate the source of the molten rock.

↑ When Mount Etna erupted in 1983, dynamite was used in an attempt to control the flow of lava. The aim of the operation was to divert the flow of lava into an inactive crater on the volcano. The men shown above are building a canal which will carry the lava to the desired crater. The dynamite is placed in a specially designed wall, which can be seen in the picture, and later blown up to create a 'path' between the lava flow and the canal, which leads to the crater.

FACT FILE

The greatest eruption

In 1815, Tambora, an Indonesian volcano, erupted leaving a caldera 6 km across. 180 cubic kilometres of rock were flung out. This is far more than Krakatau ejected, even though Krakatau was louder. The largest caldera on Earth is Lake Toba in Sumatra, Indonesia. It is 50 km long and 20 km wide.

The Hawaiian Islands

The plate that contains the Hawaiian Islands is drifting slowly over the hotspot that formed the volcanoes. Midway Island, at the western end of the chain, was the first to form. It is 27 million years old. Hawaii itself is at the eastern end and is the youngest island. It is 700,000 years old.

The greatest loss of life

The largest loss of life from a volcano happened in 1902, when Mount Pelée, on the Caribbean island of Martinique, erupted. A glowing hot cloud of lava, gases and ash poured down the mountain onto the town of St Pierre in the valley below. About 30,000 people in the town died. They had no time to escape as the avalanche raced towards them at over 200 km an hour.

Volcano reclaims island
Montserrat

Montserrat's Soufrière Hills volcano rumbled back to life in 1995 after 400 years of silence. By 1997, over 60% of the island's 11,000 people had been forced to evacuate, and many more followed. Whole villages were destroyed and many people were killed or injured by explosions and scorching lava flows.

RECENT VOLCANOES
2000
Guatemala

Over 50 people suffered burns in January, when Pacaya volcano erupted. Lava flows prompted the evacuation of thousands more.

Iceland

Hekla, one of Europe's highest volcanoes, erupted in March.

Carpets of ash 3 cm thick covered the area, turning the snowy landscape black.

Japan

In spring, Mount Usu erupted, raining ash and a stinking smell of sulphur upon nearby towns, forcing helicopter evacuations. Mount Oyama on Miyake Island then erupted eight times in two months. By September, the entire island was abandoned.

2001
Indonesia

In January and February, Indonesia's most active volcano, Mount Merapi, forced hundreds of people to evacuate, after lava and ash gushed from its crater.

Italy

Mount Etna, Europe's most troublesome volcano, was watched by the world during the summer, as several craters spewed ash and rivers and bombs of lava. Even astronauts in orbit watched the clouds from space.

The Philippines

The Philippines faced two types of volcanic disaster during the summer. Firstly Mayon volcano erupted twice in a month, pounding its surroundings with rocks and ash. Then Mount Pinatubo's water-filled crater almost collapsed. A controlled draining in September provided a narrow escape from fatal flash floods.

Ecuador

In August, Tunguraha volcano spewed clouds which blanketed the surrounding farmland in ash 10 cm deep, destroying crops.

GLOSSARY

acid rain — rain which has acid in it, formed as a result of pollution.

archaeologist — someone who pieces together history from evidence such as the ruins of buildings, statues, pottery and wall paintings.

atmosphere — the envelope of gases which surrounds the Earth.

basalt — a type of rock formed from dark, runny lava.

caldera — a huge, round crater formed when the sides of a volcano collapse, or when the top blows off during an eruption.

core — the central part of the Earth, which is made up mainly of iron. The inner core is thought to be solid and the outer core liquid and very hot.

crater — the hollow at the top of a volcano.

crust — the thin outer layer of rock around the Earth.

earthquake — a movement or tremor of the Earth's crust, often caused by plates moving against each other.

erode — to wear away rock and soil by the action of wind and rain.

erupt — to force lava and other volcanic material out through a weak place in the Earth's crust.

evolution — the way in which animals and plants slowly change over millions of years to adapt to changes in the climate or the environment, or in order to protect themselves from predators.

geologist — someone who studies the layers of rock in the Earth's crust.

geothermal — heat from inside the Earth.

global warming — the increasing Greenhouse effect, caused by the build-up of carbon dioxide and other gases in the atmosphere. This could have a serious effect on climates all over the world.

igneous rock — rock formed from hardened lava or magma.

impermeable rock — rock which water cannot seep through, such as granite.

landslide — large amounts of rock, soil and other material tumbling down a hillside.

lava — magma which reaches the surface and pours out of a volcano.

magma — the molten rock inside the Earth.

mantle — the layer of semi-molten rock between the crust and the core. The upper mantle is thought to be so hot that the rocks have melted into a liquid.

nutrients — nourishing ingredients.

plates — the sections of the Earth's crust. There are about 15 plates. Their constant movements cause changes in the Earth's surface.

pollute — to poison the air or water by allowing a build-up of substances such as waste gases.

porous rock — rock with tiny holes in it, like a sponge, which water can seep through.

pumice — light rock formed from lava with gas bubbles trapped in it.

silica — a mineral in the Earth's crust.

tuff — hardened volcanic ash.

vent — the hole in the top of a volcano through which the molten magma is forced out.

INDEX

Photocredits

Abbreviations: l-left, r-right, b-bottom, t-top, c-centre, m-middle